Flesh vs Spirit

An Intellectually Battle

CIARRA MOORE

Copyright Info

© Copyright 2017 by Ciarra Moore.

Design by Tempestt S. Smith and Antonio T. Smith, Jr. Cover photos taken Deaunna Mitchell.

ATS Publishing
2915 Avenue M 1/2
Galveston, TX 77550
www.theatsjr.com/ats-publishing

Ordering Information:
Quantity sales. Special discounts are available on quantity purchases by corporations, associations, and others. For details, contact the publisher at the address above.
Orders by U.S. trade bookstores and wholesalers. Please contact Big Distribution: Tel: (281) 816-7753 or visit www.theatsjr.com/ats-publishing

Printed in the United States of America

Publisher's Cataloging-in-Publication data
Moore, Ciarra
Flesh Vs. Spirit : An Intellectually Battle / Ciarra More
p. cm.
ISBN 978-0-9988207-2-9
Poetry

Table of Contents

Chapter 1
A Mother's Love

The first thing I think about when I wake in the morning,

Holding you close to my heart at all times baby I'm your comfort zone even when it's storming,

When I laid eyes on you within no time, well actually instantly, I knew for the first time this love in my heart was True,

The way you fill my heart with so much Joy there is no way my days will ever be sad & blue,

I looked into your little precious eyes for the first time thinking to myself How in the world did I ever make it in life without you,

Watching you peacefully sleeping every wiggle, smile, and every funny face,

Thankful that through all my bad decisions that God has redirected me while He granted me with His Mercy & Grace,

Scared out of my mind once I was aware of your existence but every great blessing has its time & place,

Now I can understand completely why a mama bear is so protective over her cub,

A feeling this special can only be a gift granted by the higher power from the man up above,

There is nothing in this world that would ever amount to the power of A MOTHER'S LOVE!

Chapter 2
Natural High

If my spirit was shook or even low,

Looking at my contacts I knew exactly where to go,

With a smile so bright and hair like snow
Jesus was the sweetest name you'll ever know,

To our family, you were the spirit, root, and pretty much the soul,

Having your family get the closest to God was your eternal goal,

When it came to protecting your family nothing could make you fold,

You ran a good race and put up a good fight,

No more suffering or pain but you gave it all your might,

While my heart is hurting I look up to the sky,

My tears stop as my smile forms thinking about you showing God your Natural High

Chapter 3

The Wave Of Her

Rather I have on makeup or torn up clothes,

I was created by God so there is nothing about me that you should ever loath,

Even with the best pair of glasses you still wouldn't see,

Deep inside my eyes to view the core of me,

A complete duet like a beach flow on the sand,

God created a perfect guy for this incredible woman,

Going through my trails but the storms I never stop fighting through?

Armor on that's so strong that I can withstand you battles too,

You're the heart of your family so love conquers any over processes thoughts of your brain,

God continuously gives you strength to not let anyone else's battles drive you insane,

You've watched me transform and I thank God for your place in my life,

With a solid foundation brick by brick, you were built strong enough to carry your family as his backbone but most importantly as your supportive the wife.

Chapter 4
Meant To Be

No one could amount to the way that cares,

When you need me the most you look up and I'm always there,

Pure beauty of a real man intricate me so pardon my stare,

Turn my back on you never could I do so it's the truth I wouldn't dare,

I'm enjoying getting myself right so no need to race,

Our fruits harvest will be sweet because we let it grow at its own pace,

Feeling weak, unwanted or foolish could never be the case,

My faith is too strong so I know that everything has its time & place,

No need to grovel over your flesh because I'm impressed if u simply just joked,

A vibe indescribable to no other because we are equally yoked,

My spirit is moved even if my flesh isn't stroked,

Feel safe and protected with you like a baby snuggled up in a sturdy crib,

God created me just to be along your right side I fit, exactly where you're missing a Rib.

Chapter 5
Lost

Such a familiar face but not sure who you are,

To be so close to you but yet feel so far,

Here in your presence but yet somehow I still feel absent,

Remembering those happy moments by now everything is like a fairytale like haze in my mind as if it were all just allusions,

Every so strange how all those great memories turned into a multitude of confusion,

An awkward feeling is stimulating my body when you touch my spine,

Unbelievably close almost as if the touch were mine,

Feeling your cool soothing breathes upon skin,

Seeing the happy ending to this story but not a clue on how the story when began,

Enjoying the closeness of our bodies side by side you I slowly inhale your scent,

Tryna feel those joyous occasions which have happened to have came & went,

An extremely faint memory that seemed as if it was just a phase,

Draining the oxygen out of my space like I was in the middle of a closed off maze,

Feels like I was buying the worlds most expensive diamond all at no cost

It doesn't feel good to anyone when the Reflexion of you happens to be LOST

Chapter 6
Mental Battle

In a house where no one else appears,

Constantly in a battle praying against my deepest fears,

Vocally muted with a continuous flow of tears,

Grateful that I've made it through such challenging times over the years,

Thinking about creating a solid foundation in my life. What could I do? Or What could I be?

Mirror moments staring for hours trying to figure out who this is that I happen to see,

Doing my very best to plant good seeds in my life so that I produce good fruit on my trees,

Thanking God daily and trusting Him with my life because He knows what's best for me,

I would rather have a heart of gold than to have a tail that rattles,

God will keep guiding me through my journey blocking obstacles in my path during each MENTAL BATTLE.

Chapter 7

Numb

Staring directly through people while my mind is deep in space,

My physical body is here but my mind is in another place,

Not knowing how to approach me because my facial expressions are blank,

In a silly mood like I'm standing in the center of an empty fish tank,

Kept my nose turnt up like I'm not lovable and my attitude stank,

Making myself unapproachable so people don't think twice about coming my way,

Face emotionless and disconnected because I have nothing to say,

Out of my space & my personal life is where you will stay.

Being hurt in so much the pain was like having a million splinters stuck in my thumb,

Removing all emotions while distance was needed for my plateau to stay NUMB!

Chapter 8
BlackOut

You've learned our culture from our home land,

In this day and age, all men are raised the same way but every male still isn't viewed as a real man,

Even if he introduces himself standing tall, hand out with his shoulders back and a straight neck,

All because of his ethnicity

What you believe he doesn't deserve no respect?

He made silly mistakes when he was younger but he made sure he got himself together at last,

He tries to live his life as a righteous man, had his life taken away without good reason but the first thing that is brought up are the things that happened in the past,

How people can just shoot to kill another person you have to have some kind of contaminated heart,

To claim you are a Christian and believe in God but you try to make your wrong doings right. I don't get that part,

Don't take what I'm saying the wrong way cause it's not to promote violence, start riots, or even for anyone to scream and shout,

I will soon have a son and these are things I must think about.

It's just extremely difficult for me to grasp the concept of others wanting other humans to not be educated and the fact that they want to take the BLACKOUT!

Chapter 9
Conquers All

Hearts are made to give love but people allow theirs to be filled with loath,

When others show hatred, dishonesty, and always full of deceit you end up learning it's the devil's work giving the wolf the sheep's clothes,

Wonders of the world are very intriguing to the thoughts of how some things are even allowed,

I have lost my way, Dear God.

I'm speaking to you here on my knees I beg of you, I am here completely broken and bowed,

Bad seeds have infested my garden so these plants I'm pulling up at the roots and my soul must be re-plowed,

My mind, my heart, and my hands are open to receive you Lord and to be filled with all of you father, please Sir, I need to be endowed,

It's mighty difficult for even me to see the sunshine Beneath the harshness of this storms ugly cloud,

When people actions come out wrong I'm working on not reaction off of impulse knowing that if I want to continue to grow I must think twice,

It's truly a brutal battle within me because it's so easy for me to be mean and aggressive instead of being kind and nice,

I will never bring the devil any joy as he smiles waiting for me to break my faith as I fall,

Allowing God to use me to strengthen my faith making me strong from the inside of my heart

Because God is love, He Conquers ALL!

Chapter 10
Son

Emotions are scattered as my skin starts to glow,

As I accept the reality of my life I mentally and physically start to grow,

Do my best to keep the root of me solid and pure so that the seeds I plant will allow me to enjoy the sweetest harvest that I could sow,

I speak greatness over your life because an awesome man is all I can allow you to be,

Teaching you values and morals with pure golden intentions so that God will bless you more than he has blessed me,

Everyday training myself to become better than I was the previous day so the greatest me is what your little precious eyes will see,

Feeling you moving and kicking, I place my hand over my growing belly thinking about how adventurous your developing brain must be and I smile,

The more my body expands the clothes I have will have to be pushed to the back of my closet for a little while, Visually noticing the changes my body has made but I definitely haven't lost my style,

Over joyed with the feeling while imagining your smile and laughter being released as you run,

Thinking of the patience I will need to have to withstand the difficulty of creating different methods that work best to provide for you to help you learn,

Doing my best to provide for you while I show love to you as well my little angel straight from my heart into yours because you are my son!

Chapter 11

I Vow

To make you fall in love with me every single day,

To help you create an easier solution when things come at us in the most challenging way,

To listen but also agree to respectfully disagree with some of the things that you might say,

To make sure you stay on Gods path for you so that you'll never be cruelly punished for things that aren't as easy for you to obey,

To not always be so serious about everything for us to keep a peace of mind at times we must have and allow our inner child out to play,

To treat you as you are a king to this queen in which we are rulers indeed in our world,

To admire and adore even the simplest things that are absolutely amazing about you as if you are a boy who is being crushed on by a little girl,

With the tenderest touch in just the right spot, you cause my toes to curl,

You giving me the best of you at all times is all I could ever allow,

On a journey to being better and getting our lives right with God daily speaking greatness over our lives on our knees and our heads, we will bow,

To submit to you while honoring what is in Gods will for us giving you unconditional love wholehearted.

Chapter 12
Lost Life

Once was my world but that love I had to let go,

Being without you and having no love for you is an emotion I never thought I'd be able to show,

On a cardiac high for a while but now it's at an all time low,

How would I ever make it without you in my life at that time I just didn't know?

The way you were to me most of the time you made me glow,

Was extremely good to you & a great harvest is what I just knew I would sow,

As time continued to go on words began to become unspoken,

The strong bond we once have shared began to be a bond that was so broken,

While I observed the change in our relationship my throat gets tight enough to cut off my airway as if I was chokin,

Giving you all that I could give you from within my heart,

You use to look at me with admiration but it had turn into a look as if I was a stank fart,

With so much love invested I would've never imagined my sanity being the cost,

There is no feeling on the world like the feeling of a love that has been lost!

Chapter 13

Snake

Smiling in my face looking right at me,

The way I'm set up I can look beyond what the eyes may see,

I laugh, smile, and joke around but ain't shit about me friendly,

You were gonna be fake or fraud, you should've just let me be,
Boasting & Bragging walking around full of deceit,

You can have your own plate but off of my plate you continue to eat,

You're forever making suggestions on where to go but it alway seems to be my treat,

With a crooked smile on your face and an extremely wicked hand shake,

Your little nasty ways you release strictly from your flesh I hope you change for your own sake,

You can't fool me cause when I look down in the grass I see your tail rattling

You ain't nothing but a Snake.

Chapter 14
Virtuous Woman

In a storm for so long, you don't know it's length,

It has rearranged your spirit, character and built up a new strength,

Once or twice I've given away my body cause I felt he urge,

Got filled with liquor so much my words are slurred,

To grow at times in your life you must do a mental purge,

Talked down to and being abused in a relationship,

Losing love and trust all at once in tainted friendships,

Could make you wanna run away or sail away on a ship,

Watching others actions over & over again as if it were a tutorial,

Ordering my steps with a husband who submits to God with me submitting to him leading our kids through the word of God are all apart of excellent morals,

Going through so many bad things becoming numb to emotions with meaningless sex becoming promiscuous finding my way back to me repenting and making this woman once again Virtuous.

Chapter 15
Her Tribute

Within so little time hearts have been broken,

So many things to say, but no words have been spoken,

Eyes wide open staring at the ceiling as I lay,

Too many mixed emotions with nothing much to say,

I do what I know how to do best so here I am on my knees I pray,

Promising Him that when times are tough I won't go astray,

As the months pass some may feel that I have dwelled too long,

But even though you know my heart doesn't mean you know it's song,

Realizing as the clock still ticks that time does still go on,

Looking up to heaven now asking him to help me be strong,

Thinking about the love I have which hurt cause you're no longer near,

Counting my calendar days to visually see that you've been gone a year.

Chapter 16

Family Tree

Divide and conquer is always the devil's plan,

But God's love is the strongest of all man,

Through the rocky road together we shall stand,

My love for you all is the bigger than anything on this land,

No one knows their place on this timeline,

We cry yet still smile & tell the next person I'm fine,

As we picture your shell beneath that dirt,

Mixed emotions surface anger, fear, heartache & hurt,

Time to end all the bad words fusses, pushes & shoves,

And extend what we know God is & that love,

Embracing who I know I am because I love the root of me,

No matter how ruffled all our branches may be Maudry
Mary Angel Sweeny loves this Family Tree.

Chapter 17

Transformations

Your mind drifts off while your body will stay,

The same thoughts & dreams are set on replay,

Constantly giving love that a lot of people don't deserve,

Becoming a prisoner of life with plenty of time served,

Trying to pitch the ball straight but somehow it keeps going at a curve,

Feeling the burn in my legs climbing the stairs to success because the stairs are steep,

Everyone wouldn't understand exactly what you're doing or saying because your intellect is too deep,

Sounds, pictures, & sweet words are all the foundation of great art,

I laugh at myself at times because I once thought that duct tape could mend my heart,

Proud of the fact that I've overcome with pain stronger than a stab from a knife or sharper than the point of a dart,

You'd be amazed at my list once I've cleaned & begun to throw unfamiliar things into my shopping cart,

In order to transform I had to dig deep to everything that hindered my spirit & let Go,

I now have a better understanding of what a wise person meant when they said if you don't get hurt you wouldn't grow,

With a transformed me I am now more mindful of the seeds that I sow,

Faith stronger than I could imagine but as small as a mustard seed causing me to have a natural glow,

Not quite sure about anyone else's journey I'm just speaking on the God I know.

You Will Never Know

Because if you put on my shoes & walked a mile,

You still won't know what it feels like behind my smile,

What you see when you look at me I'm not sure,

You could never know the extent of the pain that I've endeavored,

Stank face and sick to your stomach because of my presence, sweetheart I do hope there is a cure,

I'm strong enough to not hold on to the pain from past, If we had to switch places in life I'm quite sure you wouldn't last,

With time I've learned that my burdens aren't mine so upon God, they are cast,

As I show signs of both an extrovert and introvert it isn't fake nor is it a show,

If I could reach in my mind and give you my thoughts still YOU WILL NEVER KNOW!

Chapter 19
Back To Me

In a hurt world, lessons have been learned,

Once close friends but you know bridges do get burned,

No longer freely given, my trust must have earned,

My personal life is no longer your concern,

Being extremely loving at times causes you to be blind,

I have the right to change my mind,

Claiming to be truthful but you are constantly lying,

Learning God's word which says seek & you shall find,

Putting on a fresh pair of glasses so now I can see,

Everyone doesn't deserve to be that close to me,

Opening up new gates as I speak to him down on my knees,

Remove out of my path anyone with bad intentions please,

A real bond doesn't have to be brought or I shouldn't have to beg,

They tell you good luck followed by the statement break a leg,

Paying close attention to the words that are said,

Not soaking into my heart but analyzed carefully in my head,

Reevaluating myself as I lie in my bed,

Not in control of this path I'm going down cause by God it is led,

Open minded enough to let God do His thing because whatever will be indeed, it will be,

Willing to trust Him all on blind faith because where I am going at the moment I can't see,

Being molded by God so that I can get Back To Me

Chapter 20

Back Down

From the first time I saw you, I couldn't figure out why,

Such a charming flow with a lil playfully laid-back kinda vibe, I'm intrigued by this guy,

A vibe so connected it gives off a high as if we're levitating to the sky,

Nerve stimulation flowing through my body once our gaze was caught eye to eye,

A mixed up mind and a wounded heart's conversation bouncing around within the body can't tell them apart,

Sweetness of the simply pure connection once the temperature got hot things started to get tart,

Know that if the vibe get too strong things will go wrong so I have to keep a balance that's smart,

In a trans so strong before I even recognized it the love had become waist deep...Omg, how did this start?

As I'm watching you put your hand up your sleeves trick after trick being pulled out like kids that the party do a clown,

Even though I'm not sure as of why God's plan won't take this feeling away...

He has installed a undefeatable love it's a potluck of emotions no matter how hard I try God won't let me BACK DOWN!

Chapter 21

Your Vibe

When you look at me I don't wanna look away,

I don't want to leave cause be your side I only want to stay,

I'd rather be with you so our time together please don't neglect,

When I hug you I let my hand brush across your tender spot on your neck,

I need you to put on a show for me like you do when you perform at one of your sets,

Feeling like I hit the jackpot as I place my final bet,

We compliment each other like the perfect dress with the perfect shoe,

Goose bumps all over my body is what happens from a simple touch from you,

When you're close to me my heart skips a beat,

Fuck my knees you make me weak in the feet,

Anything on me that has stimuli you seem to stimulate,

Making me quiver in the right spot between my thighs,

Any time you like, you can just slide these panties to the side,

Pardon my french but I can't wait to feel you on the inside,

Excuse me for being so frank, but it's simply something about YOUR VIBE.

Chapter 22

In Honor of Him

As I sit here and think exactly where I should begin,

My heart smiles as I realized you've become my very best friend,

When I express my emotions all that I say is nothing less than the truth,

You invite a new life into my existence is what you do,

A supernatural feeling is what we have from the vibe I share with you,

You're so sweet opening doors and pulling out chairs,

You've shown that you caught on to the things I like even when you pulled my hair,

If my spirit is weak you listen extremely well simply because I know that you care,

If and when I ever need you I have no doubt that you'll always be there,

You're the most amazing man I've ever met which is something I constantly say,

I smile at the sky each day. Thanking God for sending you my way,

Your well being is important to me so each day for you I'll always Pray,

A genuine King who deserves to be honored especially because it's your birthday.

Chapter 23
P.U.S.H.

Divide & conquer is ultimately the devils master plan,

We shall all stick by each other because the closer we are together the stronger we stand,

It doesn't matter what happens matter because so much happens in the cruel, harsh, inhumane land,

I'll always be an open heart here to lend a genuine pure hearted hand,

If you believe that God has given His only begotten son,

He will definitely be there when times aren't so fun,

His power is stronger than the force of a bullet from a shooting gun,

God is the mightiest so when you try to dodge Him there is nowhere to run,

Can't let your faith be weak like a small, little, fragile stick,

Just trust and believe with all your heart He directs you says it in his word right in Proverbs 3 verses 5&6,

Allow yourself to be filled with him do it's out with the old and In with the new,

That won't be easy because just in that moment any sign of weakness you have opened up the devils portal right into you,

When you've reached rock bottom in your situation not knowing what else to do,

God will be there to pick you up from your trip off of the
laces on your untied shoe,

He will show you incredible things so that not only you but
others will also believe,

The faith you have doesn't have to be big it could be as
small a mustard seed,

Working your hardest to get rid of the doubt and deceit
you must first believe,

In your zone, you're reflecting as you gaze at the ceiling in
your bed stiff as a board you lay,

Wondering how loved ones lie to you right in your face but
you still let them stay,

Mental stability won't be the strongest at that point so
with you the devil will indeed have his emotional play,

But stay humble, selfless, loving, caring, genuine drop
down to your knees, Cry through all our current pain and
YOU PRAY.

Chapter 24

Unzipped Me

Something's happen in such a way in which it can't be fixed,

It's like pouring all of your water until a big pitcher that has oil at the bottom of it simply just don't mix,

When I open up my mouth I must concentrate on how my choice words are allowed to flow,

Holding back years of Water Works deep down inside as I put you through more pain to move forward my tears I had to let go,

Doing your best to use my life experiences For Your Entertainment move around sweetheart my pain is not a show,

Burying my Wounded Heart with an impersonated smile on top of all of my fake natural high,

A smooth genuine pure spirit back in the flesh you're nowhere near that guy,

Not wanting to deal with my own reality so I let my mind believe that I can fly,

Using my best defense tactics to block you out but you still entered in a way I never imagined I would see,

You've maneuvered your way past my guarded walls and reached the unzipped me.

Chapter 25

The Art of Love

So close, I slowly inhale your exhale,

I close my eyes so that I'll remember exactly how your breath smells,

So enticing my entire body has chills,

Shivers down my spine thinking about how it feels,

Your tender touch makes me smirk as you caress my skin,

An intimate mind battle that I do believe you will win,

Wanting to make the next move just give me your sign,

Flesh getting weaker and you're constantly intriguing my mind,

Such intense look as you stare into my eyes,

Got my juices flowing as your hands stroll up my thighs,

As the actions continue the temperature was normal but now it's raised above,

As we have stripped into our birthday suits, you grab your glove,

Gasp for every ounce of air as you slowly entered my Love.

Chapter 26
Undeniable Lust

Watching you disrobe made my mouth salivate,

Me & your lil guy below have a special date,

As I stare at it lustfully it change my mental state,

I have a bone to pick with him and I'm gonna set him straight,

Holding him gently as I release my spit,

As I watch it drip down there is a pulse stimulating my clit,

Slurping up the spit allowing the one to dwell in my oral walls,

But no need to stop there I keep going for the balls,

Picking up my pace as your toes curl & as you began to Run,

Deep throating you over & over til I've made you cum.

Chapter 27
The You I Never Knew

You presented yourself with such charm very gentleman like exposing you carry such a pure heart,

We could talk about any & every subject surfaced, conversations would get deep but you always find a way to say something smart,

You've always open doors & pulled out chairs proving to me that my lil meaningful gestures would make you smile but seeing you recently you looked right through me so I closed my eyes to ease the pain it hurt to feel that part,

Within good limits, a pure bond was gained while we share our hearts of gold,

That oh so inviting embrace was warm but now your shoulder has turned cold,

We use to share so many words between conversations use to flow but now all the things that you say I have to be told,

I'm fully aware that you're a nail set that seems to be missing a screw,

But I got a chance to meet with no introduction The You I Never Knew.

Chapter 28

Emptiness

On our journey to visit the wizard in oz I'm the scare crow,
I looked and seen I was missing a heart,

Emotion is shaken into a place where others weren't
allowed helping me realize you had it in your hands and
once you noticed you went to work shredding it apart,

Hurtfully heart torturing words have definitely been
wrongly spoken,

How could something so strong & beautiful carry such a
heavy load on its inside but it is easily broken,

A bitter life experience leaves a bad taste in my mouth and
a bad look on my face,

Which is a set up for a great come back for you to know
how joy taste,

Like a tire with a slow leak as time goes on, I feel myself
going down starting to deflate,

As if I was walking through the ocean in water up to my
nose and only thing keeping me afloat is my Faith,

Thoughts of you use to make me smile & blush but now
those thoughts have become the things that are causing
all my stress,

God had to detox my circle so that nothing but good
things fill up all of my emptiness.

Chapter 29

Your Old Skin

I've never let your choices affect what I am to you,

Who I present myself to be to myself as well as others is never fake I will forever stay True,

Taught myself to redirect my energy so that I am the positive wind that blows around when the devil tries to keep spirits at an all time low and blue,

You don't understand how I could not react out of anger when there are injustice actions occurring in which I don't deserve,

Even If I made a movie about my life you would never have a clue,

The way GOD created my intellectual process about matters of the world is something your brain would never have the equal opportunity to do,

Masking my internal hurt with drugs, drinking, and plenty of meaningless sex,

Guilty pleasures of the world only provide temporary comfort to the surface of oneself once the Adrenalin has faded away you are overwhelmed again with a massive amount of stress,

When your heart collaborate with your mind the guilt from all of your sinful pleasures become empowered tunneling your vision to only see the devils play on your flaws causing you to be depressed,

Carrying that the kind of weight around only makes you drag leaving you stretching yourself thin,

In order for you to renew yourself inside & out, you must detox the internal pain so that you shed Your Old Skin.

Chapter 30

Letting Go

Pushing deep down in my heart battling myself to erase those memories of you,

I don't think you have a clue about the amount of joy that you send directly to me from you,

No more moments with you like forever? What ever will I do?

Plenty of the days that passed, I wished I could just sleep to numb my heart of the thoughts of you,

When it comes to you my heart is ever so tender,

Engraved in both my heart & mind makes it super easy for me to remember,

An intellectual connection is something rare so it's one you can't take back,

An effortlessly flowing vibe How on earth do you forget that?

The hold I have on it had to loosen once it was put in my face that is maturity that you seem to lack,

A serious life situation had to take place in order for that under developed quality to show,

In my new season, a separation had to happen for us both to grow,

Whatever is meant to be will always find its way back I Trust GOD so, for now, I'm Letting Go!

Chapter 31
Miscommunicate

Tender, smooth, soft & sweet was the chemistry from start,

The way we have effortlessly flowed very well together like an expensive piece of art,

Great vibes, good times and pure happiness is what we experienced in the presence of one another people started to dis like that part,

When the vibe shared between us became visible to others the chemistry began to break my heart,

The memories that are held inside my mind I want to erase but my heart has you engraved,

Worthlessly battling to stop working for you for free self consciously I've now become your slave,

The exterior of me seem so carefree and joyous, but my interior want so badly to misbehave,

No contact with you at all is difficult to grasp but I push it into the back of my mind a lil more each day,

Me having to live without you now I never would've imagined it to be this way,

Seeing your new approach towards me after some unnecessary drama has taken my words so I'm speechless needless to say,

The vibe created a new calming peace between us like a soothing night down by the bay,

The way my heart takes my mind to a special place like they are going on a date,

When my heart keeps telling my brain things that I can't
see happen I get stuck because they've somehow
seemed to have Miscommunicate!

About The Author

Photo taken by Deaunna Mitchell for the D Marie Group,
an ATS Companies Partner

"A creative dedicated mother who has always had a passion to express herself in words in the most effective way. I have always dreamed of showing the world who I am through the collaboration of words that my heart and my mind put together. I will show the world just how amazing & fun the expression of words in can be in life.

I will be nothing less the best example for my son because I want the baseline standard of expectations in life to start with greatness so that he will grow far beyond his base line."

Learn more about Ciarra at ciarramoore.com

www.ingramcontent.com/pod-product-compliance
Lightning Source LLC
Chambersburg PA
CBHW071652040426
42452CB00009B/1838